With friendly

GREETINGS

this

CHRISTMASTIDE

1946

PRAYERS AND POEMS

PRAYERS
AND
POEMS

By

Francis Cardinal Spellman

New York

CHARLES SCRIBNER'S SONS

1946

\# 1088792

To Mary

whose only Son died that other mothers' sons
might live in love and peace

ACKNOWLEDGMENTS

For permission to reprint material which has appeared in their pages, thanks are due the following publications: *Collier's*, for "Prayer for Children"; *Good Housekeeping*, for "Sleeping Soldiers"; *Life Magazine*, for "Resurrection." Thanks are also due to The Macmillan Company, for permission to use "The Risen Soldier," originally included in the book of that title.

CONTENTS

PRAYERS AND POEMS

An American Creed

I believe in America:

In her high destiny under God to stand before the people
of the earth as a shining example of unselfish devotion to
the ideal that has made us a great nation: the Christian
ideal of liberty in harmonious unity, builded of respect
for God's image in man and every man's right to life,
liberty and happiness.

I believe in America:

For the blood in the veins of America, our heart's blood,
comes from the wounds of many peoples, chaliced in
humanity's name upon the altar of liberty.

I believe in America:

Not because of the tremendous resources of her fields and
mountains, rivers and lakes, valleys and plains, but rather
because America has been, and must ever continue to be,
the Beacon of Liberty, the Hope of the Oppressed, the
Refuge of the Weak, the Pledge and the Proof that man
can live with man in mutual respect, following God's
law, voiced in man's conscience, and in mutual esteem,
based on the responsibility of democratic life.

Lastly, I believe in America:

Because I believe in God and God's Providence that has
been over us from the earliest days of our beginnings. Believing in God, I am confident both of His merciful for-
giveness of our national sins and of His awareness of our
national virtues. Believing in God's Providence, I am
confident of our high resolve that this fair land, the vis-
ible setting of the vast, immaterial soul of the American

nation, shall never lose its initial consecration to the common Fatherhood of God, so that we and our children's children shall l e in peace and harmony among ourselves and with our neighbors. In this America, I believe; for this America, I live; for this America, I and millions of others stand ready to die.

America Reborn

Lord, lift this mighty host that is America;
Reconsecrate us in devotion to Thee.
Too oft have we forgot our heritage of faith—
The mess of pottage to our eyes was dear,
The gold within our coffers deadened us:
We, who by nature are between the earth and sky,
Earthward have sunk, and drunk of miraged visions.
But now, reborn,
We lift again to Thee our nation's soul.
Behold, we are Thy wheat,
Nurtured beneath the sunshine of the plains;
We are Thy grapes from vineyards in the sun,
And timber from Thy forests;
Ours are the iron sinews torn from earth's deep breast,
And oil from her rich arteries.

O God, we build anew and dedicate again to Thee
The host and temple of America—
Many we are, in space wide worlds apart,
But we are one today,
Made one by this, our common will:
That righteousness again shall walk among the sons of
    men.
Now, welded of our pain,
We would again be what our forebears were,
Men who did worship Thee,
And mindful of Thy Fatherhood,
Could reach to brothers o'er the sea a brother's hand.
In every man we found Thine image then,
And, finding, wrote our nation's creed,
A pledge that made us the Samaritan

To the oppressed and lowly of the earth.
In those far days, our soul was young and clear,
We opened arms to all who suffered wrong;
We bowed not, in our youth, however strong the foe,
For we were strong in loyalty to Thee,
And strong in faith that all men should know freedom
And worship Thee in freedom, as conscience should direct.

And now,
Amidst the ruins of a world that strove
To prosper and to live apart from what was bought
On Calvary by Christ, Thy Son—
Now we come back by that well-trodden way
That prodigals of every age have walked,
Back to our higher destiny—to Thee,
Our Father and our God,
And, kneeling in the valley of our grief,
Rededicate (both we who here must work
And those, our sons and brothers overseas,
Who still perhaps must die),
Rededicate ourselves to the great task that still remains,
That on the altar of our common victory,
Not to a god of war,
But to the Lord of Peace,
We give ourselves anew within the wounds
Of Him in Whom all men are one—
For all may yet redeem their faulty past,
Held in these wounded Hands of Christ, our Great High
    Priest.

We are a single host of grateful love for Thee,
A single will for universal peace for men,
A single soul of righteousness to come!
Lord, lift this mighty host that is America,
Reconsecrate us now in Thy Son's holy Name. Amen.

4

Prayer for America

O God, Father of America:
   Thou hast formed this Union of States, sealing it with
      high destiny,
   That our nation be light to all peoples in their dark
      despair,
      Life to all peoples in their fear of death,
      Love to all peoples under their yoke of hate.

For this destiny, Thou dost teach us to fly as the eagle,
   Girding us with lightning and thunder,
   Enriching us with treasures in field and fold.

O God, bless America with Thy shielding graces,
   Lest we become a nation without light, our eyes turned
      from Thee,
      A nation without life, our souls sundered from Thee,
      A nation without love, our hearts forgetting Thee.

O God, give us victory that is just, merciful and wise,
   For Thou hast chosen America to be the soul of Thy
      justice,
      The medium of Thy mercy,
      The instrument of Thy wisdom.

Let all nations know that our justice comes from Thy
      spirit,
      Our mercy from Thy heart,
      Our wisdom from Thy mind,
      Our victory from Thy strength.

Bless us, O God, with manifold graces,
    To give freely of what we have,
    To give fully of what we are,
    In victory to give ourselves alone to Thee.

O God, the Father of all nations:
    Hear our prayer for our united peoples,
    Grant guidance to our leaders, protection to our sons,
    And teach all of us Thy way of life in good will and
        peace.

Prayer for Children

How strange seems Christmas in the frame of war!
How feebly, through our dreadful night, the star
Of Bethlehem its deathless radiance shows!
How blasphemous the roar of guns and planes
Upon the silence of this sacred eve
Which Christian faith makes consecrate to Him
Who came to be the Prince of Peace, and gain,
Not by brute force, but by the might of love,
The kingdom of men's souls, with sacrifice
Divine! Deeply we believe there is no hope
For men, save in His gift of Self for them;
Nor is there love surpassing Love enshrined
In Bethlehem. For only God, Who was
Himself a Child, can light the road to peace.

We do not sense the toll of war, the price
Man pays for putting faith in force of arms,
Till we have seen war's children and their woe,
The innocent who reap of Herod's wrath.
It is the children; they are lambs of God.
They are our generation's sacrifice
For immolation on the altars raised,
Not to the loving fatherhood of God
But to the cold and cruel cult of Mars.
Dear Christ, some of the altars we have built,
With all the skill that science could command,
With all the speed our genius could beget,
Have graven golden images enshrined.
Blind hatreds fog the Tablets of the Law.
Dragon's teeth are seed for children, sired
For War's brute reaping. Cycle without end!
Once more, it is the innocent who die.

7

Oh, wilt not Thou, Who wast Thyself a Babe,
Implant in deadened souls Thy mercy's life,
That we may labor in this darksome hour
To save Thy children for a better day,
And thus ourselves be found unworthy less
Than now, of mercy at Thy Judgment seat!
Thy Spirit wrote, "A little child shall lead";
And now the day is here for Thee, a Child,
To lead us stricken peoples back to peace,
To pour within America's great soul
Desire both strong and pregnant with resolve
To save from out the ruins of our hates,
Our children, innocent of wrong. 'Tis late,
Yet this most precious gift we beg of Thee!

Somewhere—the place it matters not—somewhere
I saw a child, hungry and thin of face—
Eyes in whose pools life's joy no longer stirred,
Lips that were dead to laughter's eager kiss,
Yet parted fiercely to a crust of bread.
And since that time I walk in ceaseless fear,
Fear that the child I saw, and all the hosts
Of children in a world at play with death,
May die; or, living, live in bitterness.
Thy love, Thy Blood alone can quell man's wrath,
Thy Spirit, only, feed men's famished souls.
O Christ, have pity on Thy little ones,
From out a million broken homes they cry
To Thee, the Friend of Children, and their God.
They truly, even as Thou how long ago,
For sins that others wrought, are sentenced now.
O God, today, above the cries of war,
Hear Thou Thy children's prayer, and grant to us
Thy peace, God's peace—
                    and bread for starving children!

Prayer of Thanksgiving After Victory

O God of Destiny!
Our nation, still bleeding from the wounds of war,
Thanks Thee for the Victory of this hour,
Won by our valiant dead,
Our soldiers' blood,
Our country's tears.
We were not alone when we groped through the night of
    war,
When we drank the cup of grief,
Thou, Lord God of Hosts, wert with us,
For we were with Thee.

O God of Mercy!
Thou didst become our shield and sword,
When lawless nations rose against us.
Thou didst save us,
By Thy power that works in justice,
By Thy compassion upon our passion.

O God of Nations!
Thou hast builded this nation in a vast wilderness,
Quickening it with the blood of many peoples.
Thou hast nurtured us in a chosen land
Potent with the riches of the earth.
Thou hast made us into a mighty nation
Loving peace, yet terrible in war.

O God of Law!
Thy laws are force, ruling planet and plant,
Disposing all things mightily and gently.
Thy laws are light, guiding men's hearts and minds.

By the measure of Thy Laws nations and men wax and
wane,
For what they sow, they also reap.
Thou wilt not be mocked, O God of Law.
Make us to know and to obey Thy Will.

O God of Justice!
Repent not making of us an instrument of right,
Spending our blood, spilling it freely, curbing mad
nations.
But grant that in Victory we not offend Thy justice
By revenge, sinning against mercy,
By hate, destroying also ourselves,
Turning upon ourselves the wrath of Thy judgment.

O God of Peace!
We thank Thee that the clouds of war have lifted,
We pray Thee that the peace that comes be Thy peace,
Thy peace, which alone is our good,
A peace in obedience to Thy laws.
Thou callest us
To feed the hungry,
To clothe the naked,
To defend man's rights,
And God's rights,
And in that service,
To win back men's hearts to Thee,
And make man worthy of Thy trust in him
By man's trust in Thee.

Charity

"For Charity's sweet sake,"—these words are deep
With meaning for our deeper selves, and make
Our simplest act a consecrated thing,
Great with the greatness of a Love Divine.
For he who gives in Charity shall know
The gratitude of God and taste the cup
Of Love's inebriation, chaste and strong—
The wine of grace, which gives the soul its life.
"For Charity's sweet sake," then, let us give,
Each as the God of Love makes possible,
Not out of need or shame but with the will
That, in our war-torn hearts and stricken homes
Saddened by all the crimes and wounds of this
Our common flesh, rebellious unto God,
Love's sovereignty shall be supreme once more.

So shall we thus bind up a million wounds,
So shall we reach with hands unseen to help
The orphan who will never see, the babe,
The guiltless witness of a guilty lust;
And lift up hearts bowed down by woes unfelt
By us, who have not paid from out the purse
Of years, the price of living beyond those
Who cared that we should live. So shall we be
The strong and tender hands of Christ, the tears
Of Mary; and our prayers, by Charity
Made pure, a gift all-pleasing unto God.
Come, let us give to God this day, His bread!

Our Sleeping Soldiers

A moving scene of smiling, eager faces,
And friendly hands reached out to grasp my own,
The kneeling throngs in silent adoration
In pledge of faith, and hope in love Divine—
This is my shepherd's life, my visitation
Of far-flung pastures in a world at war.
And now with peace at dawning in these islands,
Where servitude and war have left their scars,
I think about the future's peace-crowned promise
And share with tired soldiers rest and hope.
Yet mid the happiness of war's cessation,
There lives within my soul where'er I go
The message and the memory of the fallen,
Our sleeping soldiers—hallowed be their sleep—
The multitude of men who at life's threshold,
Met death with courage, firm and unafraid.
Upon their faces fell too soon the shadows,
Too soon came nightfall and an alien grave.

They were the mighty host whose western passage
Would never know the gladness of return,
Who only from the ramparts of God's Heaven
Would see again the shrines their hearts held dear:
The sleepy main street of New England village,
The busy joyousness of old New York,
The gold-washed cuts of Colorado's canyons,
The breeze-waltzed grain of fertile Western farms,
The mystic romance of the Old South's rivers,
Her cottonwoods blanched cleanly by the moon,
The brisk, clear breathings of a Northwest morning,
And California's sun and sea-bathed shores.

These were the mystic fabric of their dreamings,
And these the scenes blurred rudely by the pain
Of men who fell asleep that nations might awaken,
That other men might live and work in peace.
Their ears, I pray, now hear a sweeter music;
Their hearts, I trust, now know a happier home;
Their minds have now a fuller understanding
Than is man's lot within this earthly world.

They rest beneath the palms whose ceaseless swaying
Is symbol of the spirit's guarding wing;
And I presume, as priest and loving brother,
Upon the tolerance of hearts inured to pain,
To pray above the graves of sleeping soldiers,
Whether in life they shared my faith or not,
And gently whisper through their death-veiled slumber:
"Soldier, I bring your mother's fondest love;
Here on your brow I place your father's blessing,
And here the love of faithful wife and child;
To you, a message from your cherished sweetheart,
For hers is sacrifice akin to yours.
Be yours the peace God grants the fallen soldier,
Whose courage gave to justice might and right,
That righteousness, through might of truth prevailing,
Again among the sons of men should dwell."

Their lives they placed upon man's noblest altar,
Entabernacled for the peace of man,
For Christian faith transmutes in man all suffering
Into eternal joys and life's awards.
And thus I feel that far beyond the living
Unto our dead my pilgrimage is made,
And in the oneness of a common sorrow,
Born of the Single Fatherhood of God,

I leave in thought the message of each dear one
Upon the altars of our templed dead.
And they in turn, to us, I feel, are speaking
With eloquence which we, the living, hear.
They ask not to have back what they have given;
They seek not praise, nor prize, nor earth's acclaim.
They only ask that we who follow after
May profit by the anguish they have borne.
They ask for men the just peace that they fought for,
The better world that they have died to build.

No Greater Love

No greater love a man can have than this,
That he should lay his life down for his friend—
Now, as I live again the varied scenes
And world-wide pattern of our fighting men,
It seems no other thought so amply fills
The measure of their sacrifice, or plumbs
So well the depth of love that has inspired
Heroic giving of themselves for us.

No greater love than this: it is a truth
Perhaps more deeply lived by some, yet lived
By all the firm and serried ranks of those
Who form a sword of light, a sword of souls,
Forged in the battle-heat of shell and bomb,
Beat out upon the anvil of our need,
Tempered by justice, and in justice drawn
Against a dreadful foe; and though it break,
Yet in its breaking is its mission won—
Even in death. These souls, this sword, shall find
The sheath of final peace, in sacrifice.

Behold the making of this mystic blade:
He was a tiny babe. His sister asked,
"Mother, he is so small, will he grow big?"
The mother smiled and kissed her baby son
Before reply: "Yes, sweetheart, he will grow,
And some day in the shadow of his strength
Many shall rest, even as you and I
Now rest within his father's kindly care."
He was a boy, just one among the throng,
The treasure-trove that is a nation's wealth—

A boy with all a boy's strange wandering ways,
Finding adventure in the fields and woods,
Turning from games to books reluctantly,
Eager to live before he sensed the price
That life would ask of him. How could he know,
As he stood daily at his desk in school,
The spark that he was nursing in his soul—
"I pledge allegiance to my country's flag,
And to the principles for which it stands,
One nation, indivisible," he pledged,
"With liberty and justice here for all."
This was the spark of freedom that would grow,
As the boy also grew, in God's good sight.
He found a world without, to which his thoughts
Within, at home, at play with other boys,
Gave glad assent. Too soon his mother found
Her son was child no more. At school, he grew
In knowledge; in the field, at sports he strove
With other boys, he worked to "make the team,"
To win the game, and learn the game of life,
Winning or losing, to play it clean and square—
And learn to win by loss as well as gain.
The boy was growing, to become a man,
Not in the mold of Nazi-Fascist thought,
But in the way America provides
For bodies' growth in strength and minds' in truth.
Then came another dawning time of hope:
As hills become apparent through a mist,
So, vaguely yet, loomed in his heart the dream—
Ideas, ideals, ambitions beckoned him,
Gave impulse to his thoughts; and in those thoughts
Was born resolve to take his rightful place,
A man, with men. Another picture stood
Upon his bureau now, another heart

16

Took place, beside his mother's, in his own,
And life and love were sweet, and home secure.

December Seventh, Nineteen-Forty-One!
A nation, that had knelt to pray, rose up
Reborn, to meet the challenge of brute force,
And from a million homes, as from the hills
The brooks break forth in spring, the young men came,
Stern-faced. Now in the fire that others lit
The precious ore of lives was forged and shaped
Into the giant blade that, swung athwart
The sky and hurtling o'er the sea, has dealt
A mightier blow, in this dark hour of war,
Than ever yet was struck by men for man.

What fire tempers hearts, what greater flame
Than hate prepared this blade? The flame of Love!
No greater gift the human heart can make
Than life itself. And so in faith we pray
That He who was Himself broken upon
The Cross will gather up and mend forever
These broken blades that we now venerate.
And that is why above the holy sod
Where these blades sheathèd rest, we place with prayer
The symbol of the Greatest Love that men
Have ever known—fired by the Flame Divine,
These found within themselves, by Heaven's grace,
A strength beyond the strength to live, a strength
Which is the strength, for what we love, to die.

Come then, let us not think of these our dead
Save only in the light of Easter morn,
For God with special love embraces those
Whose lives with Him are lived and in Him die.

Truly, in death these dear ones have found Life;
Truly, in Life our martyrs have found peace.

Some say our dead were born expendable;
In this sense only speak they true: There is
No wiser spending of this earthly span
Than, like the Master, greater love to prove
By dying for the cause one holds most dear.

The night breeze moves above our dead to-night,
To-morrow's light with warmth will touch their graves,
Yet none of them so silently shall sleep
But that the angels' lips shall o'er them breathe
The Master's benediction: Greater love
Than this no man can have, that he lay down
His life that other men may live in peace.

The Risen Soldier

❦

I am the risen soldier, I have come
From out a thousand towns, the city blocks,
The factories, the fields of this fair land
Whose name I whisper with a strange delight
Beneath these alien skies. Many am I,
Yet truly one, the son of many streams
That poured their wealth into a common cup—
The wide and golden cup of Liberty,
Which elsewhere men had sought, yet found instead
But Circe's poisoned wine, toil without sleep.
I am a soldier lifted up by War's
Stern hands and this my Nation's need, above
The petty round of pleasure; freed from wealth's
Sure chains, from labor's yoke, the snare of self,
And flung, an eagle, into atmosphere
That folds about me with immensity
Made intimate. I breast a world of clouds;
I climb, that freedom's law may find in me
A symbol of man's fondest hope, which now,
Like winter wheat, must bide beneath the chill
Of slavery, and trodden down by foes,
Dying give life to myriad golden shafts,
Each in its own true right an image clear
Of life and peace, of man with head erect,
Unbowed and fearless, under friendly skies.

I am the risen soldier; once I knew
The thraldom of a thousand little needs,
And now I have but one—the need to give

From *The Risen Soldier,* by Francis Cardinal Spellman. By permission of The Macmillan Company, publishers.

19

All that I have and am, that men may know
How fair a dream America has dreamed
Of Liberty, that now, as far as one
Lone fighter can achieve, that dream shall still
Come true for all mankind. I know that some
Will scoff and call my dream a wishful thing,
Saying wars have their origin in trade,
The ebb and flow of credit; that men are
But helpless flies within the web of commerce.
Let them drawl on if cynics they would be.
I know my soul, my heart-beats I have tallied;
Here lies my course; here gleams my compass needle.
Eastward I drive to straighten crooked crosses,
Till yet again they be the deathless sign
Of love that dies to break the bonds of man.
Westward I cleave into the setting sun,
Which still must farther set that there may be
A sunrise of Democracy and Hope
For all the lands and peoples that still lie
Within the shadows where we brought no light,
Or, when we did, too often dimmed its glow
With a fool's pride, a merchant's avarice,
Or creeds that have no room for Charity.
We could not free them, who ourselves were slaves;
We could not teach, who had not paused to learn,
Nor lead the blind, who had not eyes to see.

I am the risen soldier; though I die
I shall live on and, living, still achieve
My country's mission—Liberty in truth
And truth in Charity. I am aware
God made me for this nobler flight and fight,
A higher course than any I had deemed
Could ever be; and having found my course,

Whether I ground my plane on the home field,
Or plunge a flaming banner from the skies,
I shall not turn again to petty things,
Nor change my plan of life till God has sealed
My papers with his seal. And if it be
My blood should mingle reverently with Christ's,
His Son's, in this my final missioning,
Shall I not whisper with my dying breath—
"Lord, it is sweet to die—as it were good
To live, to strive—for these United States,
Which, in Your Wisdom, you have willed should be
A beacon to the world, a living shrine
Of Liberty and Charity and Peace."

Resurrection

Man need not wait for death, bravely to rise
From out his own dead self, and breathe a life
Renewed in deathless Christ. Oh, priceless gift,
To save ourselves in Him, and know God's love!
For as, each spring, earth's lowly things, reborn,
Quicken with sun-drawn sap and, flower-decked,
The orchards break from mourning, as the fields
The mystery of fruitfulness renew,
So does our spirit lift to nobler life,
And claim the destiny the Master set
Upon the Mount of the Beatitudes:
The life of God with men, of man in God—
One mind, one heart, one will, with the Most High.

To live our life in Christ, to share His grief,
Break daily bread with Him and find at eve,
As did disciples in the sunset glow,
The Risen Master waiting ere the dark
Encompass us, this is the Christian life—
Which truth we oft forget amid the storm
And hurried passage of these modern times.
Let us make haste—but only back to Christ;
Let us go on—but by a prayerful way;
Let us arise with all the noble souls
Who form the mighty host of God's elect,
Who heed His voice and humbly follow Him.
America has need of men like these,
Has need of men molded to Christ's own heart,
For there are murmurs in the market-place,
And strife within the councils of the mighty—
Science freezes the earth in awesome fears.

The cords of peace are in our trembling hands,
And only Wisdom can their strands unite.

Men's thoughts too oft are solely of themselves,
Our neighbors' faults we see, our own ignore,
And, blaming others as the source of ill,
Ourselves we wreck in stubbornness and greed.
O Risen Saviour, rise in us this day,
Help us to save ourselves, our country save!
This land was once a symbol of desire,
A light, a hope, to Earth's oppressed, a shrine
Where liberties, God-given, were secure.
Here, dignity clothed every man at birth;
Here, found warm welcome men from every clime,
Here man was free, where all were born to rule.
Dear Christ, let us not lose these dearly bought,
These sacred things, our liberties. Infuse
In us Thy love, quicken our nation's soul,
Lest under pretence of a better way
We find our country in the ancient snare
Of tyranny disguised in fulsome phrase.
Preserve, dear Christ, our precious heritage—
Grant us within this great, bewildered land,
A resurrection and a renaissance:
A resurrection of our truer selves,
A renaissance of all our nobler past.

In Thee, dear God, still rest our life, our hope,
And in Thy Son, the wisdom that we crave,
For even in Victory, we still need Peace:
Peace with all peoples of this wounded world,
Peace with our brothers in our strife-torn land,
Peace with our soul, the Spirit's priceless grace
These gifts, grant us today, dear Risen Christ!

DATE